WHALES

A GOLDEN BOOK · NEW YORK

Golden Books Publishing Company, Inc., New York, New York 10106

Created by Two-Can for Golden Books Publishing Company, Inc.
Copyright © 1999 Golden Books Publishing Company, Inc.
GOLDEN BOOKS®, A GOLDEN BOOK®, A GOLDEN STORYBOOK™,
and G DESIGN® are trademarks of Golden Books Publishing Company, Inc.
Library of Congress Catalog Card Number: 99-62332
ISBN: 0-307-20404-9   A MCMXCIX

World of Whales

Whales are enormous animals that swim, dive, and play in the sea. Even though they live in the ocean, whales cannot breathe underwater. They must come up to the surface to take in fresh air. Each whale has rubbery flippers and a powerful tail to help it swim.

Guess What?
Under a whale's skin, there is a layer of fat called blubber. This keeps the whale warm in cold water.

narwhal

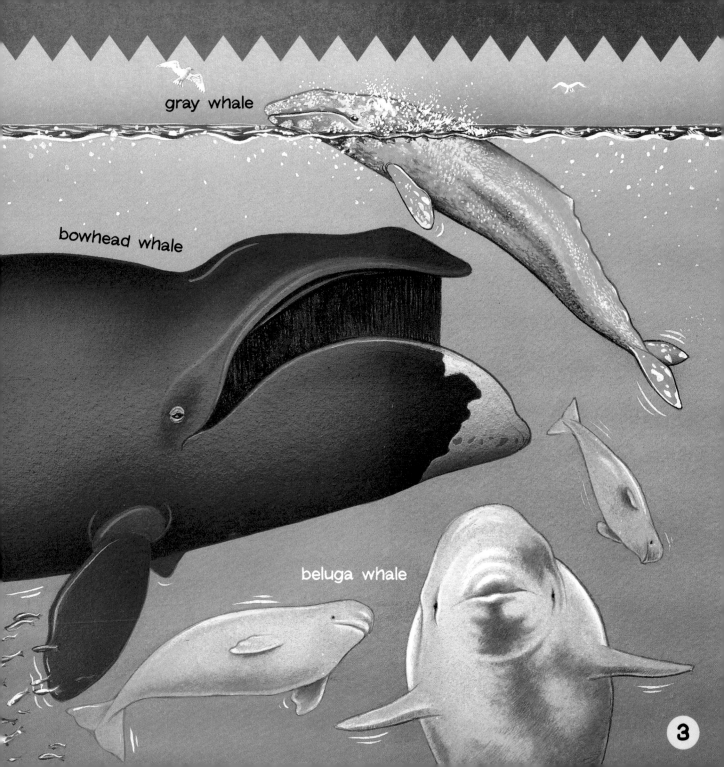

gray whale

bowhead whale

beluga whale

3

Blue Whale

The blue whale is the largest animal in the world. It lives mainly in icy seas. As this gentle giant swims along, it gulps down mouthfuls of food. Its favorite meal, called krill, is made up of tiny creatures that float in the water.

How Long?

A few blue whales have grown to 98 feet (30 m) long. That's the same length as a jet airplane.

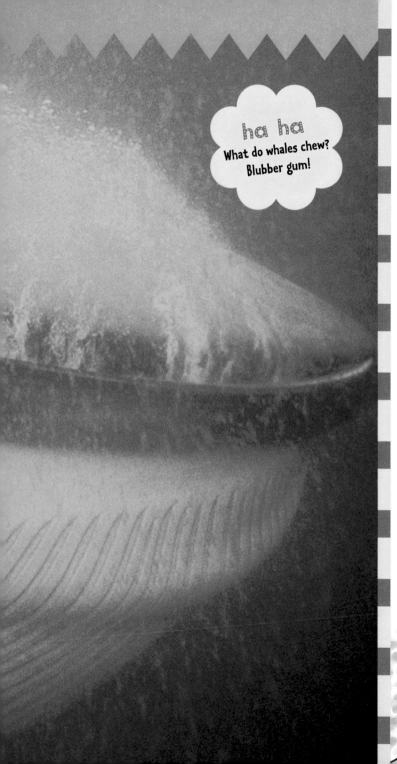

ha ha
What do whales chew?
Blubber gum!

Blue whale Facts

A blue whale's tongue is so heavy that it would take 35 strong people to lift it up.

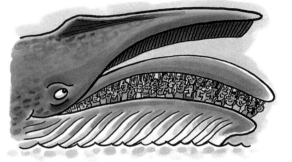

A blue whale can race along as quickly as a motorboat. Usually, though, it prefers to swim much more slowly.

Small creatures, called barnacles, glue themselves onto a blue whale's skin. The barnacles ride on the whale as it looks for food, so they can join in the feast.

Big Splash

Although a whale spends most of its time underwater, it must swim to the surface for air. Sometimes a whale splashes around in the waves before diving back down.

Tail power

When a whale dives, it throws its huge tail up into the air. Water sprays everywhere.

Riding the waves

Many smaller whales love to play in the waves made by passing boats. Some whales even leap in and out of the water in front of the boat.

There she blows!
Many whales blow tall, thin spouts,
while others blow short, fat ones.
Some whales even
blow two spouts!

Take a deep breath
A whale has either one or two blowholes,
like nostrils, on top of its head. When the
whale breathes out, it shoots a misty spray
high into the sky. This spray is called a spout.

Humpback Whale

A humpback whale is a real entertainer. Its favorite trick is to jump high into the air, then land with a tremendous splash. A humpback whale's large, bumpy head and long flippers make it easy to spot.

ha ha
How would a whale travel on land?
By whale-road!

How Heavy?

Keep out of the way of a mighty humpback whale. It's as heavy as three fire engines!

A humpback whale likes to laze around and watch the world go by. It floats on its back with its tail and flippers in the air.

Nosy humpbacks may swim up to a boat to see what's going on. The whales are so big, they often give the people on board a fright.

ARGH!

Hello!

A male humpback whale is the loudest singer in the ocean. He also can sing a song to his mate that may last for 30 minutes!

Feed Me!

Many whales have sharp teeth for catching and crunching up large sea animals. Other whales feed on tiny sea creatures, called krill. Instead of teeth, these whales have hundreds of bony strips in their mouths, called baleen.

minke whale

Guess What?
Baleen is made of exactly the same stuff as your fingernails.

A big appetite

After a minke whale takes a huge mouthful of water and krill, it closes its mouth. The water flows back out through the baleen, leaving the delicious food trapped inside.

Surfing for a snack

A fierce killer whale surfs toward the shore to look for a tasty treat. The hungry whale hopes to grab an unlucky sea lion with its sharp teeth.

A fishy trick

A humpback whale uses its blowholes to trap fish in a bubbly net. Then the whale swims toward the fish and gobbles them up.

Sperm Whale

The sperm whale is a huge and daring hunter. It dives deep into the ocean to catch lobsters, giant squid, and even fierce sharks. A sperm whale grabs one of these critters with its long, pointed teeth and gulps the animal down.

ha ha
What do baby whales play with? Doll-phins!

12

How Deep?

A sperm whale can dive as deep as a submarine. The whale may even reach the bottom of the ocean as it searches for food.

A sperm whale's favorite food is giant squid, but it munches on everything it finds— from coconuts and apples to even stones and boots!

Sperm whales have contests to prove who is stronger. They bash their heads together until one of the whales gives up.

In spring, a father sperm whale swims away and leaves his family. He spends the summer in cooler seas, where there is more food.

13

Baby Whales

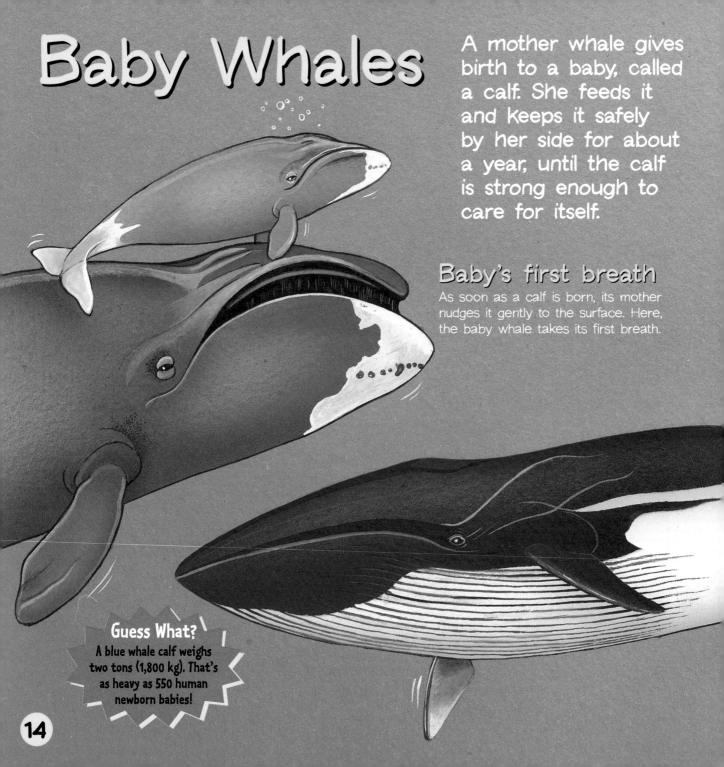

A mother whale gives birth to a baby, called a calf. She feeds it and keeps it safely by her side for about a year, until the calf is strong enough to care for itself.

Baby's first breath

As soon as a calf is born, its mother nudges it gently to the surface. Here, the baby whale takes its first breath.

Guess What?
A blue whale calf weighs two tons (1,800 kg). That's as heavy as 550 human newborn babies!

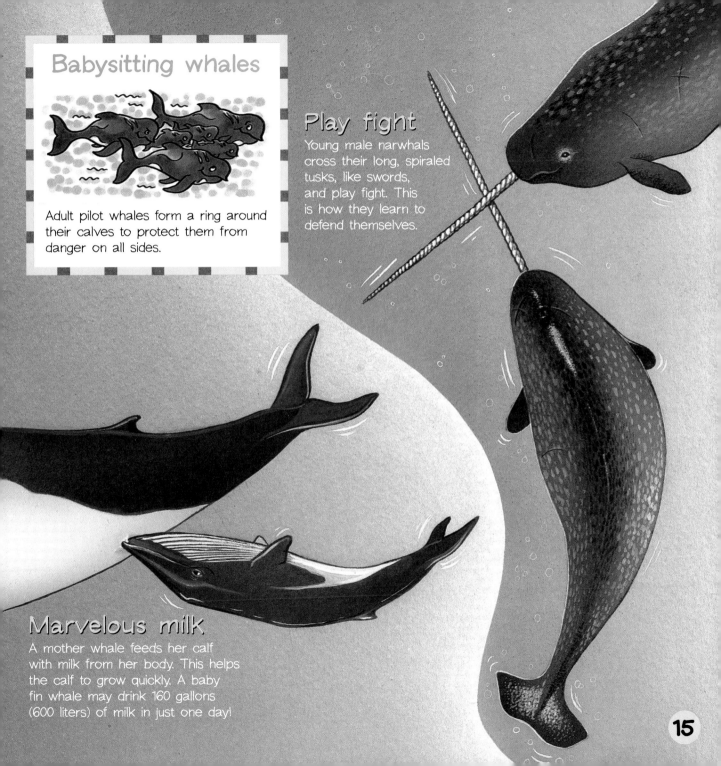

Babysitting whales

Adult pilot whales form a ring around their calves to protect them from danger on all sides.

Play fight

Young male narwhals cross their long, spiraled tusks, like swords, and play fight. This is how they learn to defend themselves.

Marvelous milk

A mother whale feeds her calf with milk from her body. This helps the calf to grow quickly. A baby fin whale may drink 160 gallons (600 liters) of milk in just one day!

Close Friends

Many whales live in groups, called herds. They swim together on long journeys and even talk to one another in their own special language.

Keep in touch

Whales talk to each other by making clicks and whistles. These sounds can travel through the water for up to 50 miles (80 km).

To the rescue

When a whale is sick or hurt, the other whales in the herd come to the rescue. They help the sick whale swim to the surface for air.

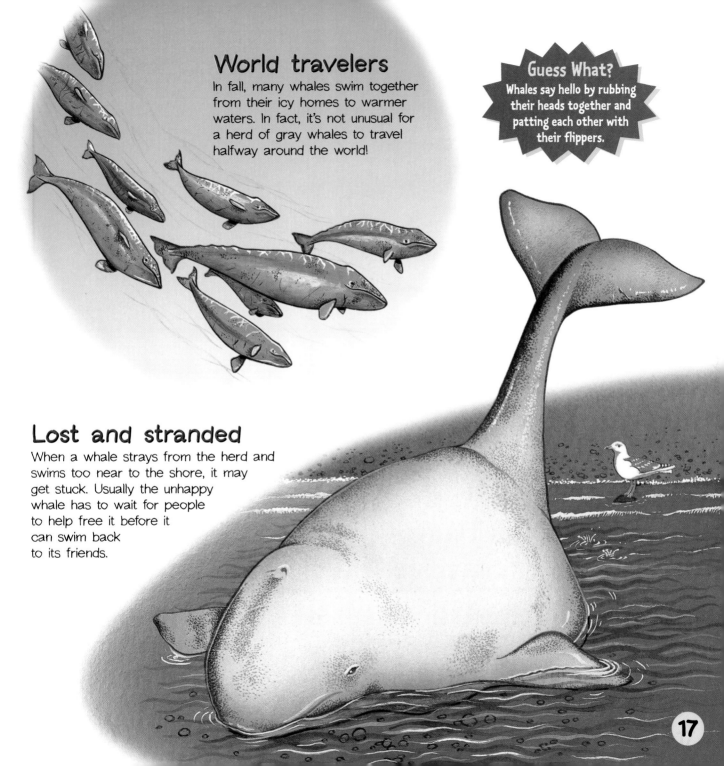

World travelers

In fall, many whales swim together from their icy homes to warmer waters. In fact, it's not unusual for a herd of gray whales to travel halfway around the world!

Guess What?
Whales say hello by rubbing their heads together and patting each other with their flippers.

Lost and stranded

When a whale strays from the herd and swims too near to the shore, it may get stuck. Usually the unhappy whale has to wait for people to help free it before it can swim back to its friends.

SAVING THE WHALES

Thousands of years ago, there were lots of whales swimming in the sea. Over time they began to die out. What went wrong?

Where is everybody?

1 In the 1800s, people hunted and caught about 10,000 whales a year. These were mostly slow-moving sperm whales, hunted for their oil.

2 People sold different parts of the whales to make all kinds of things, from candles to lipstick.

oil lamps

face cream

candles

lipstick

3 To make things worse, whales were poisoned by trash thrown into the sea. They needed help...

Cough, cough!

4 Eventually, many people let the world know that whales were in danger. In the 1930s, the first laws were made to stop hunters from harming too many whales.

SAVE THE WHALES

5 People also made parts of the sea safe for whales. Here, the whales cannot be disturbed.

ANTARCTICA

SAFE PLACE FOR WHALES

KEEP OUT!

WHALE WATCHING

Now people go on whale-watching tours. They travel all over the world to see the whales swimming happily along.

If you want to learn more about saving whales, write to SAVE THE WHALES, P. O. Box 2397, Venice, CA 90291 or visit their Website at http://www.savethewhales.org

Fast Facts

On these two pages, you can learn more amazing facts about these whales.

79 feet (23.7 m)
blue whale

Blue whale

Weight: 120 tons (109,000 kg)
Teeth or baleen: Baleen
Food: Krill
How to spot: Huge body and blue-gray skin
Amazing skill: A blue whale blows the highest spout. It can shoot spray 30 feet (9 m) into the air. That's as high as a house!
Herd size: Usually travels with 2 or 3 other blue whales

Sperm whale

Weight: 40 tons (36,300 kg)
Teeth or baleen: About 50 sharp teeth, each up to 8 inches (20 cm) long
Food: Giant squid, lobsters, and even small sharks
How to spot: Wrinkly skin like a prune and a gigantic square head
Amazing skill: Sperm whales dive really deep into the ocean to hunt for giant squid.
Herd size: May swim alone or in groups of 50 or more sperm whales

Humpback whale

Weight: 30 tons (27,200 kg)
Teeth or baleen: Baleen
Food: Krill and small fish
How to spot: A pointed, bumpy snout and especially long flippers
Amazing skill: This whale is fun to watch. It often slaps its flippers against the surface of the ocean and leaps out of the water.
Herd size: Spends most of its time with 1 or 2 other humpback whales

52 feet (15.6 m)
sperm whale

48 ft (14.4 m)
humpback whale

43 ft (12.9 m)
gray whale

26 feet (7.8 m)
killer whale

16 feet (4.8 m)
motorboat

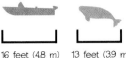
13 feet (3.9 m)
beluga whale

Gray whale

Weight: 30 tons (27,200 kg)
Teeth or baleen: Baleen
Food: Shrimp, shellfish, and worms
How to spot: Blotchy, gray skin covered in barnacles
Amazing skill: Gray whales swim farther than any other whales. A herd of gray whales may travel up to 12,000 miles (19,500 km).
Herd size: Swims alone or with several other gray whales

Killer whale

Weight: 8 tons (7,200 kg)
Teeth or baleen: About 50 curved, sharp teeth
Food: Fish, birds, seals, and even other whales
How to spot: Black body with white patches and large flippers shaped like paddles
Amazing skill: Killer whales are expert swimmers. They can leap out of the water and skim across the surface.
Herd size: Spends its whole life in a close family group of up to 25 killer whales

Beluga whale

Weight: 1 ton (900 kg)
Teeth or baleen: About 35 small, peglike teeth
Food: Fish and squid
How to spot: White body that helps it to hide in the icy waters where it lives
Amazing skill: Beluga whales chat noisily to each other. They cheep, whistle, and even roar.
Herd size: Lives with between 5 and 20 other beluga whales

Puzzles

Here are some puzzles to try. Look through the book to help you find the answers.

Close-up!

We've zoomed in on the bodies of three different whales. Can you tell which body parts they are?

Match the babies

All of these baby whales are swimming with their mothers, except for one. Can you spot the lost baby whale swimming on its own?

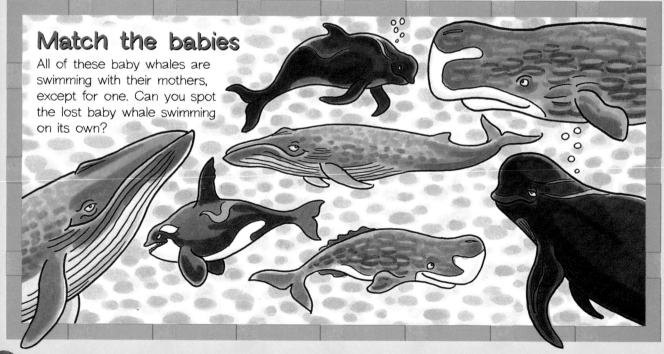

Spot the differences

Look carefully at these two pictures of a whale blowing a spout. Can you spot four differences between the pictures?

a

b

Who am I?

Do you know the names of these whales? Unscramble the letters to find out.

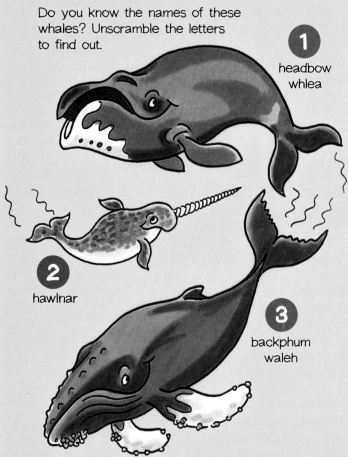

1
headbow whlea

2
hawlnar

3
backphum waleh

23

Index

Main illustrations: Miles Changeur
Cartoon illustrations: Alan Rowe
Consultant: Dr. Frances Dipper
Photographs: front cover: NHPA/Gerard Lacz;
p4: Planet Earth Pictures; p8: Bruce Coleman;
p12: Ardea London Ltd.